LEVEL
2

Penguins

Anne Schreiber

NATIONAL
GEOGRAPHIC

Washington, D.C.

To Hannah Sage and Hannah Rose
—A.S.

Published by National Geographic Partners, LLC, Washington, D.C. 20036.

Library of Congress Cataloging-in-Publication Data
Schreiber, Anne.
Penguins! / Anne Schreiber.
p. cm.
ISBN 978-1-4263-0426-2 (pbk. : alk. paper) — ISBN 978-1-4263-0427-9 (library binding : alk. paper)
1. Penguins—Juvenile literature. I. Title.
QL696.S473S37 2009
598.47—dc22
2008022879

Cover: © Frans Lanting/Corbis; 1: © Marco Simoni/Robert Harding World Imagery/Getty Images; 2: © Bryan & Cherry Alexander/Seapics.com; 4-5: © Shutterstock; 8 (left), 32 (bottom, right): © Marc Chamberlain/Seapics.com; 6-7, 32 (top, right), 32 (middle, right): © Martin Walz; 8-9: © Bill Curtsinger/National Geographic/Getty Images; 8 (left inset), 14-15: © Seth Resnick/Science Faction/Getty Images; 8 (bottom inset): © Fritz Poelking/V&W/Seapics.com; 9 (top inset), 26 (top, left): © Shutterstock; 9 (right inset): © Worldfoto/Alamy; 10-11, 14 (inset), 32 (bottom, left): © Paul Nicklen/National Geographic/Getty Images; 12: © Jude Gibbons/Alamy; 13, 32 (top, left): © Martin Creasser/Alamy; 16, 32 (middle, left): © Colin Monteath/Hedgehog House/Getty Images; 17: © Kim Westerskov/Getty Images; 18: © Maria Stenzel/Corbis; 19: © blickwinkel/Lohmann/Alamy; 20, 22: © DLILLC/Corbis; 21: © Sue Flood/The Image Bank/Getty Images; 23: © Graham Robertson/Minden Pictures; 24-25: © Paul Souders/Photodisc/Getty Images; 26-29 (background): © Magenta/Alamy; 26 (top, center), 26 (bottom, right): © Tui de Roy/Minden Pictures; 26 (top, right): © Barry Bland/Nature Picture Library; 26 (bottom, left): © Kevin Schafer/Alamy; 27 (top, left), 29 (top, left): © W. Perry Conway/Corbis; 27 (top, right): © Rolf Hicker Photography/drr.net; 27 (bottom, left): © Sam Sarkis/Photographer's Choice/Getty Images; 27 (bottom, right): © Zach Holmes/Alamy; 28 (top, left): © Konrad Wothe/Minden Pictures/Getty Images; 28: (top, right): © Tom Brakefield/Photodisc/Getty Images; 28 (bottom, left): © Ingrid Visser/Seapics.com; 28 (bottom, right): © T.J. Rich/Nature Picture Library; 29 (top, right): © Nature-photo-Online/Alamy; 29 (bottom): © Photodisc/Alamy; 29 (bottom, right): © Bryan & Cherry Alexander/Alamy; 30: © Solvin Zankl/drr.net; 31 (top, left): © Andy Rouse/Corbis; 31 (bottom, left): © Darrell Gulin/Photographer's Choice/Getty Images; 31 (right): © David Tipling/The Image Bank/Getty Images; 32 (bottom, right): © Michael S. Nolan/Seapics.com

**National Geographic supports K–12 educators with ELA Common Core Resources.
Visit natgeoed.org/commoncore for more information.**

Printed in the United States of America
Paperback: 16/WOR/9

Table of Contents

What Are They?

EMPEROR PENGUINS

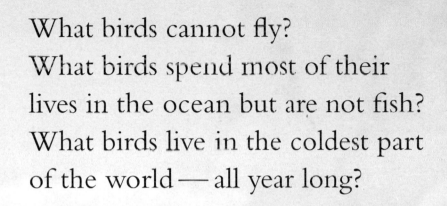

What birds cannot fly?
What birds spend most of their
lives in the ocean but are not fish?
What birds live in the coldest part
of the world — all year long?

They swim, they march, they
slide through the snow.

They are penguins.

Where Are They?

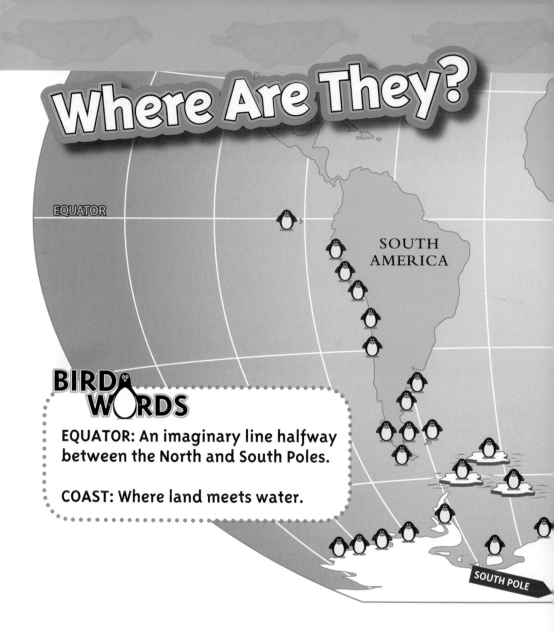

EQUATOR

SOUTH AMERICA

BIRD WORDS

EQUATOR: An imaginary line halfway between the North and South Poles.

COAST: Where land meets water.

SOUTH POLE

All penguins live between the Equator and the South Pole. Some live where it's very cold. Some live in warmer places like the coasts of Africa or Australia.

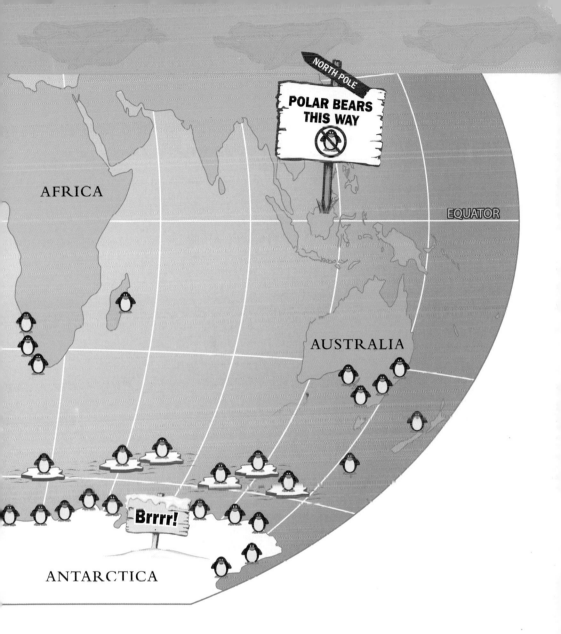

Penguins live on islands, on coasts, and even on icebergs in the sea. They just need to be near water, because they spend most of their lives IN the water.

Not Just Any Bird

EMPEROR PENGUIN

Big webbed feet for better steering.

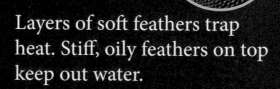

Layers of soft feathers trap heat. Stiff, oily feathers on top keep out water.

Penguins are perfect for their lives at sea. They have a sleek shape for speed. A layer of blubber keeps them warm.

Stiff flippers act like boat paddles to push and steer.

Big eyes to see underwater.

BIRD WORDS

WEBBED: Connected by skin.

9

Their black backs make them hard to see from above. Their light bellies make them hard to see from below. But it's their strong, solid flippers that help them escape predators and get where they want to go.

Penguins can swim about 15 miles an hour. When they want to go faster, they leap out of the water as they swim. It's called porpoising (por-puh-sing), because it's what porpoises do.

GENTOO PENGUINS

A predator is an animal that eats other animals.

11

What's for Dinner?

HUMBOLDT PENGUIN

Life in the ocean is fish-elicious! Penguins eat a lot of fish. They have a hooked bill, or beak, to help them grab their dinner. Barbs on their tongues and in their throats help them to hold on to slippery food.

Would you like a drink of salty water to go with that fish? Penguins are able to clean the salt out of ocean water. They get fresh water to drink and the salt dribbles back into the ocean.

BIRD WORDS

BARB: Something sharp and pointy like a hook.

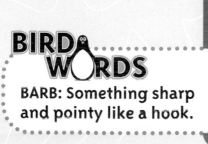

BIRD WORDS

MARINE MAMMALS: Have fur and give birth to live young; unlike other mammals, they spend most of their time in the ocean.

While penguins are slurping down their dinners, they have to be careful not to end up as dinner themselves. Penguins are the favorite food of marine mammals such as leopard seals and killer whales.

GENTOO PENGUINS AND A SKUA

Penguins are also in danger on land. Birds like the skua, the Australian sea eagle, and the giant petrel eat penguins. Even cats, snakes, foxes, and rats eat penguins when they can.

Life on Land

KING PENGUINS

BIRD WORDS

COLONY: A group of animals who live together.

On land, most penguins live in a large colony with thousands or even millions of other penguins. If it's cold, they huddle together. It's so warm inside a huddle that penguins take turns moving to the outside to cool off.

KING PENGUIN HUDDLE

Penguins march together to get to their nesting grounds. Once there they wave, strut, shake, call, nod, dance, and sing to find a mate. Most penguins stay with their mate for many years.

A Chick Is Born

CHINSTRAP CHICKS

Most penguins lay two eggs at a time, but often only one egg survives. The mother and father take turns keeping the egg warm. When it hatches, the parents keep the chick warm and fed.

ADELIE CHICKS

After a couple of weeks, hundreds or even thousands of chicks wait together while the parents go back to the sea to find food. As the chicks wait, they are in constant danger from skuas, eagles, and other animals.

KING CHICK

GENTOO FEEDING CHICK

Finally, the parents return with food. They have to find their chicks in a huge crowd of baby birds. How do they do it? The baby birds sing special songs to help their parents find them.

In a few months, the whole family returns to the sea.

The Longest March

EMPEROR PENGUINS

For the emperor penguins, getting to their nesting grounds is hard work. Their home is Antarctica—the coldest place on Earth.

Emperor penguins nest much farther from the ocean than other penguins. They must march for days and nights through snow and wind.

After laying her egg, the female gives it to the male. He will keep it warm in a flap under his belly. Unlike other penguins, the male emperor cares for the egg by himself while the female goes back to the ocean to find food.

The mother is gone for more than four months. The father huddles with the other male penguins to keep himself, and his egg, safe and warm. During this time, the father eats nothing but snow.

When the mother returns in July, the father quickly goes to the ocean to find food. By December, the whole family is ready to go.

EMPEROR PENGUINS

Penguin Parade

Galapagos
HEIGHT
18″–21″

Fairy
HEIGHT
16″
SMALLEST

Fairy penguins sing more songs than any other penguins.

Snares
HEIGHT
21″–25″

Fiordland
HEIGHT
24″

Erect-Crested
HEIGHT
24″–26″

There are 17 different species, or kinds, of penguins.

Rockhopper
HEIGHT
21"–25"

Yellow-Eyed
HEIGHT
23"–30"

These penguins are the loudest. They sound like donkeys.

Magellanic
HEIGHT
24"–28"

African
HEIGHT
24"–28"

Macaroni

HEIGHT
21″−26″

Royal

HEIGHT
24″−28″

These penguins are the fastest swimmers.

Chinstrap

HEIGHT
27″

Gentoo

HEIGHT
27″−30″

Adelie
HEIGHT
22"–26"

Humboldt
HEIGHT
22"–26"

These penguins don't make a nest.
They carry their eggs wherever they go.

King
HEIGHT
37"

LARGEST
Emperor
HEIGHT
44"

Penguin Play

HOPPING: Rockhoppers can hop five feet high!

ROCKHOPPER PENGUIN

Life isn't always easy for penguins.
But at least they look like they're
having fun.

SINGING: Adults
sing to their mates,
and chicks sing for
their parents.

MACARONI PENGUIN

SLEDDING: Penguins speed
down icy hills on their feet and
bellies to get somewhere fast.

KING PENGUIN

SURFING: Penguins surf
through the waves.
Sometimes they surf right
from the water up onto land.

CHINSTRAP PENGUIN

31

BARB
Something sharp and pointy like a hook.

COAST
Where land meets water.

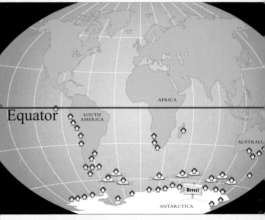

COLONY
A group of animals who live together.

EQUATOR
An imaginary line halfway between the North and South Poles.

MARINE MAMMALS
Have fur and give birth to live young; unlike other mammals, they spend most of their time in the ocean.

WEBBED
Connected by skin.